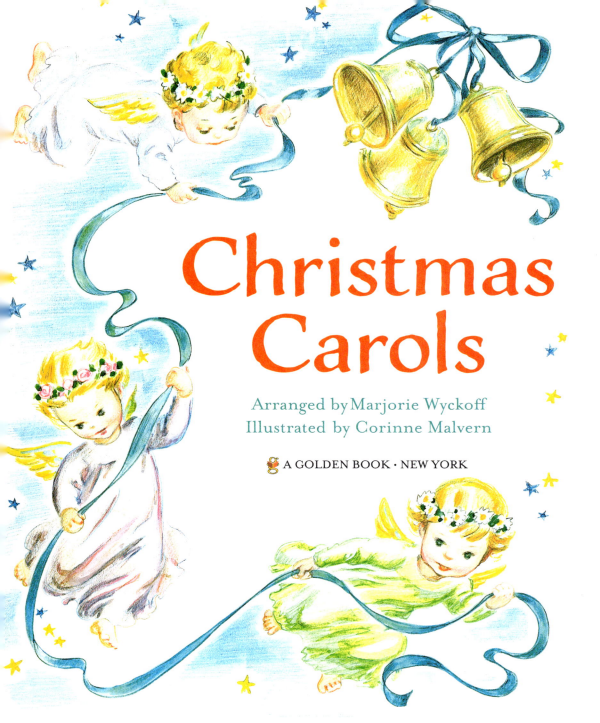

Christmas Carols

Arranged by Marjorie Wyckoff
Illustrated by Corinne Malvern

A GOLDEN BOOK · NEW YORK

Copyright © 1946 and copyright renewed 1973 by Penguin Random House LLC. All rights reserved.
Published in the United States by Golden Books, an imprint of Random House Children's Books,
a division of Penguin Random House LLC, 1745 Broadway, New York, NY 10019. Originally
published in slightly different form by Simon and Schuster, Inc., and Artists and Writers Guild, Inc.,
in 1946. Golden Books, A Golden Book, A Little Golden Book, the G colophon,
and the distinctive spine design are registered trademarks of Penguin Random House LLC.
A Little Golden Book Classic is a trademark of Penguin Random House LLC.
rhcbooks.com
Educators and librarians, for a variety of teaching tools, visit us at RHTeachersLibrarians.com
Library of Congress Control Number: 2017958795
ISBN 978-1-5247-7175-1 (trade) — ISBN 978-1-5247-7195-9 (ebook)
Printed in the United States of America
10 9 8 7 6 5 4 3

O Jesu Sweet, O Jesu Mild

Scheidt's Tablaturbuch, 1650
"O Jesulein suss, O Jesulein mild"

Harmonization (simplified) by J. S. Bach

O Jesu sweet, O Jesu mild,
Help us to do Thy holy will.
Lo, all our lives are Thine alone,
Since, in our hearts,
    Thy love has shone.
O Jesu sweet, O Jesu mild.

Away in a Manger

Martin Luther *German Folk Song*

See the blazing Yule before us,
Fa, la, la, la, la, la, la, la, la.
Strike the harp and join the chorus,
Fa, la, la, la, la, la, la, la, la.

Follow me in merry measure,
Fa, la, la, la, la, la, la, la, la.
While I tell of Yuletide treasure,
Fa, la, la, la, la, la, la, la, la.

The First Nowell

Words Traditional   *Traditional English Melody*

The first Nowell the angel did say Was to certain poor shepherds in fields as they lay; In fields where they lay keeping their sheep, On a cold winter's night that was so deep.

Refrain
Nowell, Nowell, Nowell, Nowell, Born is the King of Israel.

O Come, All Ye Faithful

Anonymous Latin Hymn, 17th or 18th Century
Translated by Fred. Oakley, 1841

J. F. Wades Cantus Diversi, *1751*

O come, all ye faith-ful, joy-ful and tri-umph-ant, O come ye, O come ye to Beth - le - hem;

O Christmas Tree

Ernst Anschütz, after a 16th-Century Folk Song *Traditional German Tune*

He Is Sleeping

George Wolfson

Polish Carol, 16th Century
Arranged by Marjorie Wyckoff

Chil - dren, come and see Him slum - ber, In the man - ger soft with hay. He, our bless - ed lit - tle

I Saw Three Ships

Traditional English   *Traditional Air from Derbyshire*

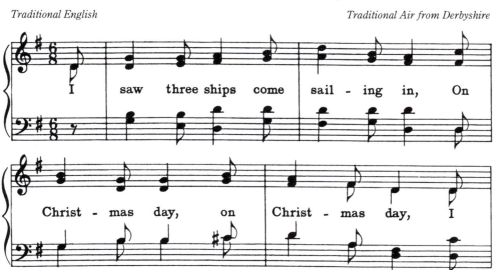

I saw three ships come sail-ing in, On Christ-mas day, on Christ-mas day, I